THE INCOGNITO LOUNGE

THE INCOGNITO LOUNGE

AND OTHER POEMS

DENIS JOHNSON

CARNEGIE MELLON UNIVERSITY PRESS
PITTSBURGH 2007

Acknowledgments

"The Incognito Lounge" was first published in *Antaeus*.
"Boarding," "The Story," "Nude," and "Surreptitious Kissing" were published in
Poetry.
"The Confession of St. Jim-Ralph" first appeared in *Raccoon*.
Other selections appeared in the following periodicals: *The American Poetry
Review*, *The Iowa Review*, *Ironwood*, *Missouri Review*, *Skywriting*, and *Sonora
Review*.

The Incognito Lounge was originally published by Random House and selected
by Mark Strand for the National Poetry Series in 1982.

First Carnegie Mellon University Press Edition, February 1994;
Second Edition, February 2007

The publisher expresses gratitude to James Reiss
and James W. Hall for their contributions to
the Classic Contemporaries Series.

to the people I have lied to

The author is most grateful to the Book-of-the-Month Club, the National Endowment for the Arts, and the Arizona Arts Commission for gifts that made these poems possible.

CONTENTS

One

Two

ONE

THE INCOGNITO LOUNGE

The manager lady of this
apartment dwelling has a face
like a baseball with glasses and pathetically
repeats herself. The man next door
has a dog with a face that talks
of stupidity to the night, the swimming pool
has an empty, empty face.
My neighbor has his underwear on
tonight, standing among the parking spaces
advising his friend never to show
his face around here again.
I go everywhere with my eyes closed and two
eyeballs painted on my face. There is a woman
across the court with no face at all.

———————————

They're perfectly visible this evening,
about as unobtrusive as a storm of meteors,
these questions of happiness
plaguing the world.
My neighbor has sent his child to Utah
to be raised by the relatives of friends.
He's out on the generous lawn
again, looking like he's made
out of phosphorus.

———————————

The manager lady has just returned
from the nearby graveyard, the last
ceremony for a crushed paramedic.
All day, news helicopters cruised aloft
going whatwhatwhatwhatwhat.
She pours me some boiled
coffee that tastes like noise,
warning me, once and for all,
to pack up my troubles in an old kit bag
and weep until the stones float away.
How will I ever be able to turn
from the window and feel love for her?—
to see her and stop seeing
this neighborhood, the towns of earth,
these tables at which the saints
sit down to the meal of temptations?

———————

And so on—nap, soup, window,
say a few words into the telephone,
smaller and smaller words.
Some TV or maybe, I don't know, a brisk
rubber with cards nobody knows
how many there are of.
Couple of miserable gerbils
in a tiny white cage, hysterical
friends rodomontading about goals
as if having them liquefied death.
Maybe invite the lady with no face
over here to explain all these elections:
life. Liberty. Pursuit.

———————

Maybe invite the lady with no face
over here to read my palm,
sit out on the porch here in Arizona
while she touches me.
Last night, some kind
of alarm went off up the street
that nobody responded to.
Small darling, it rang for you.
Everything suffers invisibly,
nothing is possible, in your face.

———————

The center of the world is closed.
The Beehive, the 8-Ball, the Yo-Yo,
the Granite and the Lightning and the Melody.
Only the Incognito Lounge is open.
My neighbor arrives.
They have the television on.

It's a show about
my neighbor in a loneliness, a light,
walking the hour when every bed is a mouth.
Alleys of dark trash, exhaustion
shaped into residences—and what are the dogs
so sure of that they shout like citizens
driven from their minds in a stadium?
In his fist he holds a note
in his own handwriting,
the same message everyone carries
from place to place in the secret night,

the one that nobody asks you for
when you finally arrive, and the faces
turn to you playing the national anthem
and go blank, that's
what the show is about, that message.

———————————

I was raised up from tiny
childhood in those purple hills,
right slam on the brink of language,
and I claim it's just as if
you can't do anything to this moment,
that's how inextinguishable
it all is. Sunset,
Arizona, everybody waiting
to get arrested, all very
much an honor, I assure you.
Maybe invite the lady with no face
to plead my cause, to get
me off the hook or name
me one good reason.
The air is full of megawatts

and the megawatts are full of silence.
She reaches to the radio like St. Theresa.

———————————

Here at the center of the world
each wonderful store cherishes
in its mind undeflowerable
mannequins in a pale, electric light.

The parking lot is full,
everyone having the same dream
of shopping and shopping
through an afternoon
that changes like a face.

But these shoppers of America—
carrying their hearts toward the bluffs
of the counters like thoughtless purchases,
walking home under the sea,
standing in a dark house at midnight
before the open refrigerator, completely
transformed in the light . . .

———————

Every bus ride is like this one,
in the back the same two uniformed boy scouts
de-pantsing a little girl, up front
the woman whose mission is to tell the driver
over and over to shut up.
Maybe you permit yourself to find
it beautiful on this bus as it wafts
like a dirigible toward suburbia
over a continent of saloons,
over the robot desert that now turns
purple and comes slowly through the dust.
This is the moment you'll seek
the words for over the imitation
and actual wood of successive
tabletops indefatigably,
when you watched a baby child

catch a bee against the tinted glass
and were married to a deep
comprehension and terror.

WHITE, WHITE COLLARS

We work in this building and we are hideous
in the fluorescent light, you know our clothes
woke up this morning and swallowed us like jewels
and ride up and down the elevators, filled with us,
turning and returning like the spray of light that goes
around dance-halls among the dancing fools.
My office smells like a theory, but here one weeps
to see the goodness of the world laid bare
and rising with the government on its lips,
the alphabet congealing in the air
around our heads. But in my belly's flames
someone is dancing, calling me by many names
that are secret and filled with light and rise
and break, and I see my previous lives.

ENOUGH

The terminal flopped out
around us like a dirty hankie,
surrounded by the future population
of death row in their disguises—high
school truant, bewildered Korean refugee—
we complain that Bus 18 will never arrive,
when it arrives complain what an injury
is this bus again today, venerable
and destined to stall. When it stalls

at 16th and McDowell most of us get out
to eat ourselves alive in a 24-hour diner
that promises not to carry us beyond
this angry dream of grease and the cries
of spoons, that swears our homes
are invisible and we never lived in them,
that a bus hasn't passed here in years.
Sometimes the closest I get to loving

the others is hating all of us
for drinking coffee in this stationary sadness
where nobody's dull venereal joking breaks
into words that say it for the last time,
as if we held in the heavens of our arms
not cherishable things, but only the strength
it takes to leave home and then go back again.

NIGHT

I am looking out over
the bay at sundown and getting
lushed with a fifty-nine-
year-old heavily rouged cocktail
lounge singer; this total stranger.
We watch the pitiful little
ferry boats that ply between this world
and that other one touched
to flame by the sunset,
talking with unmanageable
excitement about the weather.
The sky and huge waters turn
vermilion as the cheap-drink hour ends.
We part with a grief as cutting
as that line between water and air.
I go downstairs and I go
outside. It is like stepping into the wake
of a tactless remark, the city's stupid
chatter hurrying to cover up
the shocked lull. The moon's
mouth is moving, and I am just
leaning forward to listen
for the eventual terrible
silence when he begins,
in the tones of a saddened
delinquent son returned
unrecognizable, naming

those things it now seems
I might have done
to have prevented his miserable
life. I am desolate.
What is happening to me.

HEAT

Here in the electric dusk your naked lover
tips the glass high and the ice cubes fall against her teeth.
It's beautiful Susan, her hair sticky with gin,
Our Lady of Wet Glass-Rings on the Album Cover,
streaming with hatred in the heat
as the record falls and the snake-band chords begin
to break like terrible news from the Rolling Stones,
and such a last light—full of spheres and zones.
August,
        you're just an erotic hallucination,
just so much feverishly produced kazoo music,
are you serious?—this large oven impersonating night,
this exhaustion mutilated to resemble passion,
the bogus moon of tenderness and magic
you hold out to each prisoner like a cup of light?

THE BOARDING

One of these days under the white
clouds onto the white
lines of the goddamn PED
X-ING I shall be flattened,
and I shall spill my bag of discount
medicines upon the avenue,
and an abruptly materializing bouquet
of bums, retirees, and Mexican
street-gangers will see all what
kinds of diseases are enjoying me
and what kind of underwear and my little
old lady's legs spidery with veins.
So Mr. Young and Lovely Negro Bus
Driver I care exactly this: zero,
that you see these things
now as I fling my shopping
up by your seat, putting
this left-hand foot way up
on the step so this dress rides up,
grabbing this metal pole like
a beam of silver falling down
from Heaven to my aid, thank-you,
hollering, "Watch det my medicine
one second for me will you dolling,
I'm four feet and det's a tall bus
you got and it's hot and I got
every disease they are making

these days, my God, Jesus Christ,
I'm telling you out of my soul."

THE SONG

The small, high wailing
that envelops us here,
distant, indistinct,

yet, too, immediate,
we take to be only
the utterances of loose fan

belts in the refrigerating
system, or the shocked hum
that issues from the darkness

of telephone receivers;
but it speaks to us
so deeply we think it

may well be the beseeching
of the stars, the shameless
weeping of coyotes

out on the Mohave.
Please.
Please, stop listening

to this sound, which
is actually the terrible
keening of the ones

whose hearts have been broken
by lives spent in search
of its source,

by our lives of failure,
spent looking everywhere
for someone to say these words.

THE WHITE FIRES OF VENUS

We mourn this senseless planet of regret,
droughts, rust, rain, cadavers
that can't tell us, but I promise
you one day the white fires
of Venus shall rage: the dead,
feeling that power, shall be lifted, and each
of us will have his resurrected one to tell him,
"Greetings. You will recover
or die. The simple cure
for everything is to destroy
all the stethoscopes that will transmit
silence occasionally. The remedy for loneliness
is in learning to admit
solitude as one admits
the bayonet: gracefully,
now that already
it pierces the heart.
Living one: you move among many
dancers and don't know which
you are the shadow of;
you want to kiss your own face in the mirror
but do not approach,
knowing you must not touch one
like that. Living
one, while Venus flares
O set the cereal afire,

O the refrigerator harboring things
that live on into death unchanged."

They know all about us on Andromeda,
they peek at us, they see us
in this world illumined and pasteled
phonily like a bus station,
they are with us when the streets fall down fraught
with laundromats and each of us
closes himself in his small
San Francisco without recourse.
They see you with your face of fingerprints
carrying your instructions in gloved hands
trying to touch things, and know you
for one despairing, trying to touch the curtains,
trying to get your reflection mired in alarm tape
past the window of this then that dark
closed business establishment.
The Andromedans hear your voice like distant amusement park music
converged on by ambulance sirens
and they understand everything.
They're on your side. They forgive you.

I want to turn for a moment to those my heart loves,
who are as diamonds to the Andromedans,
who shimmer for them, lovely and useless, like diamonds:
namely, those who take their meals at soda fountains,
their expressions lodged among the drugs
and sunglasses, each gazing down too long
into the coffee as though from a ruined balcony.

O Andromedans they don't know what to do
with themselves and so they sit there
until they go home where they lie down
until they get up, and you beyond the light years know
that if sleeping is dying, then waking
is birth, and a life
is many lives. I love them because they know how
to manipulate change
in the pockets musically, these whose faces the seasons
never give a kiss, these
who are always courteous to the faces
of presumptions, the presuming streets,
the hotels, the presumption of rain in the streets.
I'm telling you it's cold inside the body that is not the body,
lonesome behind the face
that is certainly not the face
of the person one meant to become.

TWO

NUDE

My luck has been so all but
perfect I can imagine
nothing that might be added

save perhaps one or two more
such truly astonishing
visions as these fine hairs—

blossoms, really, these little
originations of life in
the parched world, this excellent

sparse grove that is lucked on,
never sought and found, just here
above the navel, just here where

I touch for one second
and then I must recover.
Also, if my good luck is not

yet quite too far beyond
that prudently afforded
my sort, I would like

to have several more
of these buttocks, precisely
duplicated, naturally

presenting as it fades this pale
impression of my fingers
on the left one. And may I have

the bodies with them, too? This
is actually the most unnerving
and celestial of girls, it's

not enough that she was in
the living room now as I entered,
why couldn't she have been in

the room I just left, as well
as all the other rooms at once?
Do you see what foul lurches

underproduction leaves us in?
And so suppose this girl were
to become lost? Lost! Would you

want to witness my running
into all the rooms exclaiming
year after year Whatever

shall I do? Lately I have been
noticing how everything
loved must reach the touch

of grief to the lover—it is
an unusual prize geranium
that does not die—but perhaps

one or two more of this girl,
of course with these arresting—
oh, my, these prosecuting

and sentencing!—thin arms,
each finely braceleted or
just plain covered with twenty-

dollar bills, emeralds, alarm
devices and this bewildering
soft skin could be managed?

VESPERS

The towels rot and disgust me on this damp
peninsula where they invented mist
and drug abuse and taught the light to fade,
where my top-quality and rock-bottom heart
cries because I'll never get to kiss
your famous knees again in a room made
vague by throwing a scarf over a lamp.
Things get pretty radical in the dark:
the sailboats on the inlet sail away;
the provinces of actuality
crawl on the sea; the dusk now tenderly
ministers to the fallen parking lots—
the sunset instantaneous on the fenders,
memory and peace . . . the grip of chaos . . .

THE STORY

Dunking one
adjacent a disturbed
old woman in the elevated
train station donut shop,
you think: Heavenly lady,

I'm drinking coffee
and you're dripping mucus,
is that the story?—but say nothing,
fearing either reply. Curious
days, these, spent

in fear of replies, in horror
of doorways, sleep, friendships,
and what napkins!—wordless
white interrogations wanting
the whole story, again,

from the beginning;
napkins like the vast, anemic
dawns that find you awake
by the window, trying to
remember how it goes,

failing: the disastrously loved
one's face some Martian's
now, the swell architecture of the old

houses similarly permutating
in memory's half-light,
and boxes?—What
can you do save drift
motherless through these tears when
the cardboard box remembers
the legend of the distant

store in a cool dry place
where all are freed of desire
and change, the fat man
simply standing, selling
nothing, the others silent,

every edge gleaming
with the perfect, acrylic veneer
of reality? But does a box
dream, or is it you who dreams,
and is this truly a dream of reality

or only a memory of sanity?
Turn around. Look back. Now
remember: there they drank wine
with you a last time,
there they cried with you a last time,

now the shelter is only a hailstone
that fell there,
for already they've folded away the voices,
already they've put away the light,
now that this one

whom we told
nothing
goes away saying I hear your words,
I will seek these things,
I will know by these signs.

SURREPTITIOUS KISSING

I want to say that
forgiveness keeps on

dividing, that hope
gives issue to hope,

and more, but of course I
am saying what is

said when in this dark
hallway one encounters

you, and paws and
assaults you—love

affairs, fast lies—and you
say it back and we

blunder deeper, as would
any pair of loosed

marionettes, any couple
of cadavers cut lately

from the scaffold,
in the secluded hallways

of whatever is
holding us up now.

FROM A BERKELEY NOTEBOOK

One changes so much
from moment to moment
that when one hugs
oneself against the chill
air at the inception
of spring, at night,
knees drawn to chin,
he finds himself in the arms
of a total stranger,
the arms of one he might move
away from on the dark playground.

Also, it breaks the heart
that the sign revolving like
a flame above the gas
station remembers the price
of gas, but forgets entirely
this face it has been
looking at all day.
And so the heart is exhausted
that even in the face

of the dismal facts we wait
for the loves of the past
to come walking from the fire,
the tree, the stone, tangible
and unchanged and repentant

but what can you do.
Half the time I think
about my wife and child,
the other half I think how
to become a citizen

with an apartment, and sex
too is quite on my mind,
though it seems the women
have no time for you here,
for which in my larger, more
mature moments I can't blame them.
These are the absolute

pastures I am led to:
I am in Berkeley, California,
trapped inside my body,
I am the secret my body
is going to keep forever,
as if its secret were
merely silence. It lies
between two mistakes
of the earth,

the San Andreas
and Hayward faults,
and at night from
the hill above the stadium
where I sleep,

I can see the yellow
aurora of Telegraph
Avenue uplifted

by the holocaust.
My sleeping
bag has little
cowboys lassoing bulls
embroidered all over
its pastel inner
lining, the pines are tall
and straight, converging
in a sort of roof

above me, it's nice,
oh loves, oh loves, why
aren't you here? Morgan,
the pyjamas are so
lonesome without
the orangutans—I write
and write, and transcend
nothing, escape
nothing, nothing
is truly born from me,
yet magically it's better
than nothing—I know

you must be quite
changed by now, but you
are just the same, too,
like those stars that keep

shining for a long time after
they go out—but it's just a light
they touch us with this
evening amid the fine
rain like mist, among the pines.

ON THE OLYMPIC PENINSULA

Stranger, to one like you,
here only the old
people feel like talking—
but abruptly, as if already in the midst
of talk, as if they sensed
with you a kinship in closeness
to endings—and you aren't kind
with them. Stranger,
here the sea doesn't obliterate,
but just lies there carved up
into bays and inlets, indolent
or waiting. In the town's one
hip bar the lesbians lean
into sinister embraces, dancing
together and speaking just softly
enough that you can't hear. Your girl
is gone and you are here
because you think maybe they
have taken her from you
into this establishment where the men
stink like murdered sea animals;
they have flying beards, black
mouths they spill the beer
into over their laughter
so that you think of someone urinating on coals.
Sometimes you unexpectedly taste
the inside of your own mouth, choking

as you kiss this bitter foreigner,
and you feel yourself forgetting, even as you remember,
that you've gone strange and everybody
else is happy and just having
good clean fun in a place where the ocean
is large and cares nothing for men,
that you are an image of blood
graven amid peace and wine,
a strange one,
claustrophobic and heart-stopped among
garden parks through which boys
jog perspiring in their red basketball
shorts and in which toddlers
in blue parkas on toy horses rock themselves,
already stupefied, toward oblivion.

A WOMAN

There's nobody here
but you, sitting under
the window at the corner
table as if waiting
for somebody to speak,
over your left shoulder the moon,
behind your head a vagina,
in pencil, emblazoned
above a telephone number.
For two hours you've been
looking across the street,
quite hard, at the grand store,
the Shopper's Holiday felled
across the sunset.
It grows dark in this climate
swiftly: the night
is as sudden and vacuous
as the paper sack the attendant
balloons open with a shake
of his scarred wrist,
and in the orange parking
lot's blaze of sulphur
arc lamps, each fist
of tissue paper is distinct,
all cellophane edged
with a fiery light that seems
the white heat of permanence

and worth; of reality;
at this hour, and in this
climate where how swiftly
the dark grows, and the time comes.

NOW

Whatever the foghorns are
the voices of feels terrible
tonight, just terrible, and here
by the window that looks out
on the waters but is blind, I
have been sleeping,
but I am awake now.
In the night I watch
how the little lights
of boats come out
to us and are lost again
in the fog wallowing on the sea:
it is as if in that absence not many
but a single light gestures
and diminishes like meaning
through speech, negligently
adance to the calling
of the foghorns like the one
note they lend from voice
to voice. And so does my life tremble,
and when I turn from the window
and from the sea's grief, the room
fills with a dark
lushness and foliage nobody
will ever be plucked from,
and the feelings I have
must never be given speech.

40

Darkness, my name is Denis Johnson,
and I am almost ready to
confess it is not some awful
misunderstanding that has carried
me here, my arms full of the ghosts
of flowers, to kneel at your feet;
almost ready to see
how at each turning I chose
this way, this place and this verging
of ocean on earth with the horns claiming
I can keep on if only I step
where I cannot breathe. My coat
is leprosy and my dagger
is a lie; must I
shed them? Do I have
to end my life in order
to begin? Music, you are light.
Agony, you are only what tips
me from moment to moment, light
to light and word to word,
and I am here at the waters
because in this space between spaces
where nothing speaks,
I am what it says.

THREE

TEN MONTHS AFTER
TURNING THIRTY

We've been to see a movie, a rotten one
that cost four dollars, and now we slip
in a cheap car along expensive streets
through a night broken open like a stalk
and offering up a sticky, essential darkness,
just as the terrible thing inside of me,
the thick green vein of desire or whatever it was,
is broken and I can rest.
Maybe in another place and time, people
drive slowly past the taverns
with black revolvers reaching from their windows,
but here in the part of night where every
breath is a gift tremendous as the sea,
thousands of oleanders wave
blossoms like virgins after a war.
I can hear my own scared laughter coming back
from desolate rooms where the light-bulbs
lunge above the radios all night,
and I apologize now to those
rooms for having lived in them. Things
staggered sideways a while. Suddenly
I'm stretched enough to call certain of my days
the old days, remembering how we burned
to hear of the destruction of the world,
how we hoped for it until many of us were dead,
the most were lost, and a couple lucky

enough to stand terrified outside the walls
of Jerusalem knowing things we never learned.

IN A LIGHT OF OTHER LIVES

It's raining, and the streetlights on the wet
street are like regurgitated lights,
but the ambulance's ruby element
can move among our rooms without a care,
so that we who generally sleep
where it is black awaken in a red
light of other lives, saying I
can see every article,
I can see every article in its fame.
Saying How long do I stay here in the jail
of times like this, where the clear
water has the flavor of thirst
and the meat tastes like it is eating me
and the day's bread changes into a face?
Where sometimes you see the sorrow of a whole life
open away from you white as an invitation
on the blue of night, and the moon is a monster?
All the night long I can betray myself in the honky-tonk
of terror and delight, I can throw away my faith,
go loose in the spectacular fandango
of emergencies that strum the heart
with neon, but I can't
understand anything. It is coming:
the curtains of rain and light the arc lamps
let down on First Avenue will be parted,
and from behind them, the people we really are will step out
with abandon, as if asked to dance—

the myriad tickets will fall away from the face
and the visions of the heart be delivered up naked
and lucid as teeth, and each
of the things that catch up with this robber
will fall on God: now *You* must follow
the spoor of Your own blood among
edifices, among monuments, until the police
have You in their arms
and make You say Your name.
I want to be there when the little pool of light
falls on the identification,
I swear I will never tell the others if You whisper
to me what this moment is before the ambulances,
and what these moments are
when all that was impending
begins, when the whole
downtown, arrested like a lung
between intake and expulsion, erupts
into genuineness—as if many
bells have been struck and what
the world is, is that I can touch
their ringing. It is unbreakable.
It is the examiner before whom the emptiness
inside me perjures itself.
It is the examiner who is a fist.

FOR JANE

At left, with a net, in a light
like whiskey, you skim flotsam
from the water.
I can't tell you how vivid
this undertaking is—
you are as unsettling
and as naked as that yellow
flower admiring you as it rests
along the surface of the pool.
I am just going to listen
to the sound of liquid,
the sound of oleanders.

If ever
I was about to speak I
forget. I can see
that the single flower goes
aloft on the water of
the pool because it is something
that everything has addressed
to my darling, while I stand
here like some ashes
that used to be a clown,
looking out quietly
from my face to watch the failure
of these words to be those things.

SWAY

Since I find you will no longer love,
from bar to bar in terror I shall move
past Forty-third and Halsted, Twenty-fourth
and Roosevelt where fire-gutted cars,
their bones the bones of coyote and hyena,
suffer the light from the wrestling arena
to fall all over them. And what they say
blends in the tarantellasmic sway
of all of us between the two of these:
harmony and divergence,
their sad story of harmony and divergence,
the story that begins
I did not know who she was
and ends *I did not know who she was.*

THE CIRCLE

for Jane, after a dream

I passed a helicopter
crashed in the street today,
where stunned and suddenly grief-torn
passers-by tried to explain
over and over, a hundred ways, what
had happened. Some cried over the pilot,
others stole money from his wallet—
I heard the one responsible for his death
claiming the pilot didn't need it any more,
and whether he spoke of the pilot's
money or his life wasn't clear.
The scene had a subaqueous timbre
that I recognize now as a light
that shines in the dreams I have when I sleep
on my back and wake up half-drowned.
However I tried to circumnavigate
this circus of fire and mourning—
the machine burst ajar like a bug,
the corpse a lunch pail
left open and silly music coming out—
I couldn't seem to find a way
that didn't lead straight to the heart of the trouble
and involve me forever in their grief.

THE WOMAN IN THE MOON

for Glenna K., 1922–1979

Who wouldn't have been afraid
of your face?—watching me
from another world through your cheap
frame on the dresser, while your daughter
wept and I made hysterical
love to her, trying
to banish your ghost that wandered
with its smashed head through this life
I never invited you to.
Who wouldn't have wanted to drive you out of her,
seeing how your memory, grown
sharp as flint in grief, carved
her face a little more every
day into yours?
I thought you were watching me out of her eyes,

I thought every night I heard the telephone
clatter to the floor again,
and your daughter
scream so she couldn't stop.
And for months afterward
you came to me like
nobody—secondhand,
through a daughter's hindsight,
her unblinking, horrified love,
as night

after night the room filled
with the dark and the air
burned with your murdered presence,

until I couldn't possibly make love to the dark gold
woman, vessel of your self, the torn
strings of your motherhood dripping
from her like an ocean
where she drowned but couldn't die.
Who would drag us before some tribe of elders
to be scorned,
or have anything but pity
on us, that we turned to other lovers
and lost each other?
Glenna,

forgive me: tonight, in a moment
of learning that is as clear
and absolute as ice, and hurts
as much to be inside of,
I see how much like him
I've become, the man
who beat you until you died with something
they never found—
walking in an anger of love
and hatred through these streets
just as the geraniums

of light around the baseball
diamonds are coming on—
oh, God, inside me I carry a black

night you climb through like
the moon in which the Asians
see a woman:
higher

and smaller, Glenna, farther
and farther away,
and nothing
will ever bring you back.
And nothing will ever get rid of you.

THE FLAMES

In 1972 I crossed Kansas on a bus
with a dog apparently pursued to skinniness
painted on its side, an emblem
not entirely inappropriate, considering
those of us availing ourselves
of its services—tossed
like rattles in a baby's hand,
sleeping the sleep of the ashamed
and the niggardly, crying out
or keeping our counsel as we raced over the land,
flailing at dreams
or lying still. And I awoke to see
the prairie, seized by the cold and the early hour,
continually falling away beside us, and a fire
burning furiously in the dark: a house
posted about by tiny figures—
firemen; and a family
who might have been calling out to God
just then for a witness.

But more than witness, I remember now
something I could only have imagined
that night: the sound of the reins breaking
the bones in the farmer's hands
as the horses reared and flew back into the flames
he wanted to take them away from.
My thoughts are like that,

turning and going back where nothing wants them,
where the door opens and a road
of light falls through it
from behind you and pain
starts to whisper with your voice;
where you stand inside your own absence,
your eyes still smoky from dreaming,
the ruthless iron press
of love and failure making
a speechless church out of your dark
and invisible face.

FOUR

MINUTES

You and I—we agitate
to say things, to dress every gash
with a street address or a relative.
We are found in the places of transport at an hour
when only the criminals are expected to depart.

We are blind and we don't know that our mouths
are moving as we place a hand to stay
the janitor's mop—*I'll tell you the story*
of my life, you'll make a million—
blind and we don't know that our parents are dead

as we enter the photo-booths.
In there is the quiet like the kernel of a word:
in there everything we were going to say
is taken from us and we are given
four images of ourselves. What are we going

to do with these pictures? They hold
no fascination for the abandoned,
but only for us, who have
relinquished them to the undertow
that held us, too, but let us go,

so that the hospitals opened like great vaults
for us and we stepped from bed to bed

on the faces of the diseased, the beloved,
moving like light over a necklace
of excruciations—*I'll tell you*

the story of my life,
you'll make a million . . .
this is what it means to be human,
to witness the heart of a moment like a photograph,
the present standing up through itself relentlessly like a fountain,

the clock showering the intersection with minutes
even as it gathers them to its face
in the so often alluded
to Kingdom of Heaven—
to watch one of those minutes open

like a locket and brandish a picture
of everyone we ever loved who drowned,
while the unendurable generosity of everything
sells everything out. Would you like
to dance? Then here, dance with the terror

that now is forever,
my feet are stumps. The band is just
outbreaking now with one that goes
all the evidence / the naughty evidence / persuades
the lovers endearing by the ponds /

the truants growing older in the sleazy arcades /
there's no banishing / of anything /

only con- / quering within /
make it enough / make it enough / or eat
suffering without end

THE COMING OF AGE

Outside the spring
afternoon
is occurring, my love,
just as our voices
are going home from us
to the plains, and the shapes
of ourselves, as we impose
them on this one, prepare
to blend with other
afternoons, possibly in
this very room
as tiny dusts uplifted
in the bands of sunlight,
or in other still chambers.
I don't want you to be afraid
as we stand here losing
our lives, unable to speak,
soon to enter the dream
of once having touched
this portion, that smoothness
of flesh now buried dead
and having heard the lovely
tones ascending on a voice
merely speaking; there is
the chance there will be
the singing of the voiceless,
unraveling into the unenclosed

emptiness a silence
drawn taut so
slowly its
high music encounters
us before
it begins, and we are dancing.

YOU

You were as blind to me
as your footprints last Friday,
but I saw you dancing
with that girl who wasn't me—
because I don't dance
and laugh in that terrible
style with every stranger.
But you are no stranger.

But you were strange when you were dancing,
and the room turned all yellow
and the glass I was holding
spilled burgundy wine.
I got out by the side door
and I leaned on a box,
and I saw you at the end
of every street,

and in the Flame Inn
I watched the men shooting
eight-ball and mule-kicking
the jukebox till it worked.
On the wall they had many,
many wooden plaques
bearing humorous sayings
that I will never say
to you even if you begged me,

not even if you came out
of a prison, and begged me.

POEM

There was something I can't bring myself
to mention in the way the light
seemed trapped by the clouds,
the way the road dropped
from pavement to dirt and the land from pine
to scrub—
the red-headed vultures on dead animals,
the hatred of the waitress breaking

a cup and kicking the shards across the café
that looked out on the mountain and on the white smear
of the copper mine that sustained these people.
I claim there was something you wouldn't
have wanted to speak of either,
a sense of some violent treasure
like uranium waiting to be romanced
out of the land . . .

They sat under white umbrellas,
two or three together, elbows on card tables
at the dirt roads leading to the mines,
rising each at his turn to walk
around a while with a sign
announcing they were on strike,
their crystalline and indelible
faces in the hundred-degree
heat like the faces of slaughtered hogs,

and God forgive me,
I pulled to the side of the road and wrote this poem.

RADIO

He bears a rakish feather
through the streets in a hat
on his head and has had
several drinks, and is crying.
He totters at the change
of traffic lights.
I do not know if he has just
been orphaned, or what.
From a room above the stores
the insistent test-tone
of the Emergency Broadcasting
System stares at him, and he
cannot stop hearing it.
The perfectly desolate afternoon's
single utterance is this sound
like an ambulance across
the mild lake whose driver
swims while the siren cries.
It is putting the man
in the feathered hat at
the intersection under arrest.
I do not know if he has just
been informed, or what.
I know it is my radio, but
I am only beginning to understand
whose orphanhood, whose tears.

TOMORROW

I take
you by your arm of stained glass
while the moon turns warm and wet
as the kitchen window of a distant
restaurant in the beautiful
moments after closing,
and we walk up and down—
oh! don't we promenade?
Every radio in the town
plays the same station through doorways
thrown wide to the elements and we are
buoyed and relayed how tenderly along
this underground railroad of tuneful oldies.
It is a nighttime filled
with animals, bubbles, tiny lights.
Now we do not fear treachery,
now we are not asking ourselves how
will we know if the insect lies,
how will we know if the fire lies.
The ache of our loving just
throttles us speechless inside the midnight,
though the radios are all crying out
that the weather tomorrow in
the mountains will be unprecedented.

THE CONFESSION OF
ST. JIM-RALPH

Our Patron of Falling Short,
Who Became a Prayer

I used to sneak into the movies without paying.
I watched the stories but I failed to see the dark.
I went to college and drank everything they gave me,
and I never paid for any of that water
on which I drifted as if by grace until
after the drownings, when in the diamond light
of seven-something A.M., *as the spring was tearing*
me up in Cartajena, only praying
on my knees before the magnifying ark
of the Seventh St. Hotel could possibly save me,
until falling on my face before the daughter
of money while the world poured from the till
brought the moment's length against the moment's height,
and paying was what I was earning and eating and wearing.
This to the best of my recollection
my uncle said in 1956,
moving against my father like a bear
on fire as the evening of his visit
killed the rum. He'd come from Alaska
or some place like that, the Antarctic, maybe,
and he left in a hot rage, screaming by the door
that nothing would save me from my awful father,
just as he, my uncle, had been saved

70

by nothing. Thirteen weeks from then, he died.
"This family's full of the dead," my father told me.
I was eight. I used to make excuses
to join him in the washroom as he bathed
in the mornings, soaping himself carefully
so as not to splash the automatic pistol
wrapped in plastic he rested near to hand.
At a certain point, the sun came through the blinds
and shafted the toilet bowl, filling it with light
as he spoke of killing everyone, often taking
the pistol from its wrap and holding its mouth
against his breast, explaining that no safety
lay anywhere, unless he should shoot the fear
that stood up on its hind legs in his heart.
Such things were always on TV—I thought
that one world merged in the next, and I resolved
to win the great Congressional Medal of Honor,
to make a name on the stage, and die a priest.

In the war the bullets yanked the fronds
from palms and the earth ate them up like acid
before our eyes. When dead men hit the ground
they came alive, they spoke in tongues, holding
babies that came from nowhere in their arms.
We were all afraid of the earth. My father's fear
turned it like a plow, delivering
dogs and bugs, bright music, and a feminine
whispering of our names. My comrades fled,
but I was healed by everything that happened,
the midnight Rapid Transit stations
of hand grenades made moonlight as I moved

from life to life, getting off and shouting
whatever the signs said, getting on again,
received like lightning, changing everything.
My body disappeared. The enemy
knew me as a ghost who dropped a shadow
the size of night and turned the air to edges.
I am your grand companion of surprise,
big-time harbinger cancelling everyone's
business in a constant dream of all
the starring roles and franchises the great
Congressional Medal of Honor winners win.
Wounded twice, then decorated more
than any other in my regiment,
I stood at home plate, vomit on my blouse
and whiskey in my blood, and heard the dirt
of my home town falling grain by grain
out of the afternoon, while everyone's
rahrahrahs affected me like silence.
The mayor handed me a four-by-four-
inch cardboard box a colonel handed *him*;
I threw it at the vast face of the crowd,
screaming I wanted only the Medal of Honor . . .
I lose the thread of my existence here.
I see me strange and drugged against my will,
telling my life story to a room,
traveling the aisles of an asylum
out there in Maine, among the aborigines.
They must have set me loose, or I escaped:
I see myself in a forest-bordered field,
unchanged and wearing my uniform—
free; yet somehow jailed by old desires

and saying what a soldier says: For home,
nothing. Comrades, for you, these hoarded rations.

With four monstrosities in uniforms
like mine, I pulverized guitars and wept
for the merriment of many. Brothers,
when shadows lengthen, and they lower down
the American flag and close our government,
another country rises like a mist
by garbagey coliseums on the warehouse
side of town to listen to that rock
and roll: God speaking with the Devil's voice,
unbreathable air of manacles, a storm
to bless your multicolored lips with sperm.
We sundered them until they brought their bones
forth from the flesh and laid them at our feet,
screaming their lungs shut tight as fists,
shedding their homes forever, leaving name
and tongue and mind and sending us their heads
through the mails in the night. We ran it past the edge,
we gave them something everyone could dance to—
whatever is most terrible is most real—
the Bible fights, the fetuses burning in light-bulbs,
the cunnilingual, intravenous
swamp of love. Three times I died on stage,
and the show went on while doctors snatched
me back from Chinatown with their machines.
We struck it rich. Without a repertoire,
without a name or theme, we toured the land
and eighty thousand perished. We were *real*,
but not one company recorded us:

everywhere we went they passed a law.
We toured the land—sweet, burning Texacos,
the adrenaline darkness palpitates frantically,
the highway eats itself all night, the radio's
wheedling bebop fails in the galactic
soup near dawn; the Winnebago shimmers,
everything tastes like puke, the eight-ball
bursts, nobody
knows how to drink in this fuckin town . . .
One night I heard our music end
abruptly in the middle of a number
and looked around me at a gigantic silence.
I felt the pounding, saw the screams, but all
was like the long erasure of a wind
calming and disturbing everything
on its route through stunned fields of hay.
My bodyguards tried with huge gentleness to lead
me off, but I threw myself outside, rolling
through a part of town I'd never seen—
the flat grey streets looked Hebrew, and the windows
held out the paraphernalia of old age,
porcelain Jesuses gesturing from the shadows
of porcelain vases, surrounded by medicines.
A rain began. I strained myself to hear
the trashcans say their miserable names,
but nothing. At the brink
of stardom high over the United States,
untouchable as God but better known,
I stumbled over streets that might've been rubber,
deaf as a cockroach, finished as a singer.

Brothers, I spilled myself along the roads.
Mold grew on me as I dampened in alleys.
I began in ignorance. How could I know
that whoever is grinding up his soul is making
himself afresh? That the ones who run away
get nearer all the time? Look here or there,
it's always the horizon, the dull edge
of earth dicing your plan like a potato.
Does water break the light, or light the water?
Which do you choose: what is or what is?
I painted myself black and let that color
ride through virgins like the penises
they dream of while their fathers sleep. I lied.
I cheated like a shark. I robbed the dead.
Nothing healed me, just as nothing healed
my uncle of himself—but he was healed,
while I grew phosphorescent with a kind
of cancer that I carried like a domino,
a tiny badge discovering me . . .
Oh please my love I want to rock and roll with you
Feel it feel it
feel it all night like a shoe . . .
Ten years I wasted all I had, and then
ten years I lived correctly—held a job
in a factory that made explosions,
where deafness was an asset. I did well,
I never missed a day, I polished late,
honed my skills, received promotions—in the end
I built explosions for atomic bombs,
forty-three I built myself, which one of these

days will deafen you, as I am deafened.
I wrenched the fraternal orders with my tale
of sorrowful delinquency—the Elks,
the Lions, Moose; those animals, they loved
the crippled rock'n'roller with the heart
wrung out as empty as his former mind,
and variously and often they cited me.
I walked the malls with an expanded chest,
took my sips with my pinkie cocked,
firing dry martinis at my larynx
and yearning for the strength of soul it takes
to suck a bullet from an actual
pistol, hating my own drained face
as I intimidated mirrors, or stood
in a jail of lies before the Eagle Scouts,
an alarm clock going off inside an alarm clock
in a lump of iron inside a lump of iron:
hating myself for having become my father.
At night I prayed aloud to God and Jesus
to place me on a spaceship to the moon—
Heaven, I told Them constantly, my mind
is tired of me, and I would like to die.
Take me to ground zero take me to ground zero
where in the midst of detonation it is useless
to demonstrate quod erat demonstrandum,
this was my ceaseless prayer, until my lips
were muscles and my heart could talk,
telling it over and over to itself;
until they fired me and drove me to the edge
of things, and dumped my prayer into the desert.
Drinking cactus milk and eating sand,

I wandered until I saw the monastery
standing higher and higher, at first a loose
mirage, but soon more real than I was.
There I fell on my face, and let light carry
me into the world—just as my uncle told it
nine million years ago when I was eight—
and the prison of my human shape exploded,
my heart cracked open and the blood poured out
over stones that got up and walked when it touched them.
High in the noon, some kind of jet plane winked
like a dime; I saw it also flashed
over the vast, perfumed, commercial places
filled with stupid but well-intentioned people,
the wreckages and ambushes of love
putting themselves across, making it pay
in the margins of the fire, in the calm spaces,
taken across the dance-floor by a last romance,
kissing softly in a hallucination strewn
with bus tickets and an originless music—
and now death comes to them, a little boy
in a baseball cap and pyjamas, doing things
to the locks of the heart . . . This was my vision.
Here I saw the truth of the horizon,
the way of coming and going in this life.
I never drifted up from my beginning:
I rose as inexorably as heat.

Brothers, I reached you, and you took me in.
You saw me when I was invisible,
you spoke to me when I was deaf,
you thanked me when I was a secret,

and how will I make of myself something
at this hour when I am already made?
Never a famous hero, a star, a priest—
my mind decides a little faster than
the world can talk, and what I dreamed was only
the darker sketch of what I would become.
It's 1996. I'm forty-eight.
I am a monk who never prays. I am
a prayer. The pilgrim comes to hear me;
the banker comes, the bald janitors arrive,
the mothers lift their wicked children up—
they wait for me as if I were a bus,
with or without hope, what's the difference?
One guy manipulates a little calculator,
speaking to it as to a friend. Sweat
is delivered from its mascara,
sad women read about houses . . .
and now the deaf approach, trailing the dark smoke
of their infirmity behind them as they leave it
and move toward the prayer that everything
is praying: the summer evening a held bubble,
every gesture riveting the love,
the swaying of waitresses, the eleven television
sets in a storefront broadcasting a murderer's face—
these things speak the clear promise of Heaven.

PASSENGERS

The world will burst like an intestine in the sun,
the dark turn to granite and the granite to a name,
but there will always be somebody riding the bus
through these intersections strewn with broken glass
among speechless women beating their little ones,
always a slow alphabet of rain
speaking of drifting and perishing to the air,
always these definite jails of light in the sky
at the wedding of this clarity and this storm
and a woman's turning—her languid flight of hair
traveling through frame after frame of memory
where the past turns, its face sparking like emery,
to open its grace and incredible harm
over my life, and I will never die.